Social Fluency: Genuine Social Habits to Work a Room, Own a Conversation, and be Instantly Likeable... Even Introverts!

By Patrick King

Dating and Social Skills Coach at www.PatrickKingConsulting.com

Social Fluency: Genuine Social Habits to Work a Room, Own a Conversation, and be Instantly Likeable... Even Introverts!

Introduction

1. Social fluency is learned.

2. Overcoming your social fears and excuses.

3. Social body over mind.

4. Familiarity breeds social comfort.

5. Turn social fluency on like a light switch.

6. The buddy system isn't just for swimming.

7. The barista is your guinea pig.

8. Storytelling as influencing.

9. Act familiar, become familiar.

10. Understand and take advantage of conversation patterns.

11. Conversations as pure entertainment.

12. Be unapologetically you.

13. Figure out your social triggers.

14. What you say doesn't really matter.

15. Condition emotional attraction.

16. Own group discussion dynamics.

17. Genuine social habits.

18. Take control of your feedback loops.

BONUS – The ONE exercise to instantly improve your social confidence.

Conclusion

Cheat Sheet

Introduction

I'll never forget the day I met *Janice*.

Partially because she was one of the most beautiful women I'd ever seen in real life... but mostly because I was flabbergasted that she was actually interested in me.

Despite my profession these days, I'm what you'd call a **late bloomer**. It took a while to come out of my shell and become truly comfortable with my identity, while simultaneously striving to improve all aspects of it.

Naturally, college was not an experience I'd describe as ideal, as I was just seeing other guys succeed socially and with women in ways that I could only dream of. Coincidentally, I feel that this experience allows me to be that much more effective in my line of work, as I can commiserate with exactly what they are feeling.

So when I met Janice, I was in no way, shape or form prepared for her. I was bookish, poorly dressed, and much more introverted than I am now. Despite her plethora of options, she opted to take an interest in me and apparently saw my diamond in the rough.

She asked me out for a drink and I readily agreed by telling her that I was free the next two weeks, not even knowing how to hide my eagerness. To her credit, things between us were great... when we were alone. I was truly comfortable with her and overcame many insecurities to open myself up to her. She was incredibly understanding and empathetic.

But once we took the leap of introducing each other's friends, the relationship was noticeably strained in a way that I couldn't figure out at first. I distinctly remember feeling invisible when we were out with her friends, even to her. If there was a hole in the ground, I would have jumped into it in a second, and not because of her friends, who were nice as could be.

I just didn't possess the *social habits* necessary to successfully connect with people and navigate social situations at that point. I didn't know how to connect with others on a deeper level than the weather, and it became all too apparent that it was *Janice's superior social habits* and focused effort that even allowed us to be dating in the first place.

As soon as I made that realization, she did too... and she was gone shortly thereafter.

A difficult lesson learned, but a lifetime of perspective gained.

I eventually learned that my social outcomes are truly 100% within my control, and that placing dependence on someone else to carve out a spot at the table for you – that's a losing proposition. I had to develop the social habits I wanted for myself, and discovered that they are the key to everything I wanted in life. The results were huge, and the mindset was empowering.

It's about taking the leap into the anxious and unpredictable, as social situations can often appear.

Scratch that, it can be scary as hell sometimes. But as the book title promises, *genuine social habits*, ones that reflect positively on your character and aren't manipulative or just cheerleading, can change your life.

Each social choice we make can either be aimed at furthering a genuine social habit on the path to social fluency, or it can be empty. Embrace intentionality and put in the work... and working a room, owning a conversation, being instantly likeable will be **inevitable side effects**. And that's social fluency.

With bulletproof social habits, it doesn't matter that you won't always have witty words cued up. You'll be able to fall back on cultivating the best version of yourself, and that never fails to attract others. Small talk be damned – social habits allow you to convey the type of person you want without even saying a word!

Thanks Janice, for being the best thing to barely happen to me.

1. Social fluency is learned.

If you've ever met a salesperson who you know was just *killing* it commission-wise, you'll probably know the feeling I refer to below.

They've got a certain smoothness about them that puts people at ease, and it feels like they can charm their way into anyone's good graces in record time.

This is some next level charisma and social fluency, because even though you're aware they're a salesperson and have a singular goal in mind, they don't appear like they're selling anything at all... until you return home with a shopping bag full of Gorilla Glue.

They just seem to have that *it factor* that draws people to them and allows them to adapt to any kind of conversation signal from others.

Above all else, all of their behaviors and habits seem to flow so *naturally*...

Stop right there.

Yes, it's amazingly tempting to believe that such people are just born with the gift of gab, and that you can never attain those heights for yourself.

This is remarkably and completely wrong, and as I'll discuss later, an all-too-common excuse we tell ourselves. If you were to interview any of the people that you would label as possessing social fluency, I'm positive that they would all tell you that it's something they've worked on consciously.

Maybe it's always been a strength of theirs, but that doesn't mean that salesman just woke up with the ability to sell ice to an eskimo. There's a reason that the salesman probably wasn't young and green – more experience and practice, and practice makes perfect.

This is wonderful news for you because this is the exact reason you bought this book… in the hopes that such skills were learnable, right? To gain actionable items and steps to improve your social fluency?

Good, because <u>social success is learned behavior</u>.

One more time. Social success? Oh yeah, it's learned.

At our most basic level, human beings learn by watching. As the old saying goes, "Monkey see, monkey do." We learn by imitation, modeling and observation.

It's how babies learn to walk, talk, and interact with the world. And as adults, if we watch how the fattest monkey gets all of his bananas, we can eventually learn his methods and prosper in the same way.

This is an important realization because if you're not enjoying the kind of social fluency and success that you want, it's because you have simply modeled your behavior on the **wrong** patterns and role models. All you have to do is reset some patterns, model off new behaviors, and you're on your way to everything that social fluency can do for you.

Unfortunately, humans are also creatures of habit.

It's incredibly easy for us to become stuck in our ways once we establish some semblance of working patterns. We stick with them because it's a ton of work to seek out new patterns… and we're scared that anything new won't work as well as what we currently have. You also see this type of behavior in relationships, friendships, jobs, and anything else that requires taking an iota of risk in our lives.

But once you're aware of this modeling behavior and the simple cause and effect, you should be able to more easily shift your frame of reference to observing social behaviors after those that you would want to copy.

You can sure as hell improve yourself in each and every way that you want… no one is born being able to deliver a speech like Martin Luther King, Jr. Just don't expect it to be easy, and recognize that you'll have to break down years of habits and preconceived notions.

But nothing worth having in this life comes easily, does it?

Luckily, this process gets easier with time because as with all learning and conditioning, it becomes subconscious after a certain point. You notice behaviors that get positive outcomes, and you take note for later without even noticing.

But before we get there, try the following experiment. Go out with a socially fluent friend of yours into a high stress social setting. I'm talking about a super loud bar, a situation where you know almost no one, or even a club.

Then just sit back in a corner with a drink and watch your friend. Don't tell them what you're doing or else they'll get self-conscious and won't act as they normally do.

Watch how they navigate the room. Look at their eyes, their face, and how their mannerisms change from each person they are talking to. How they include everyone and confer comfort easily. Notice how they adjust their behavior based on the direct external stimuli they receive and how they react to it.

Learn which behaviors and habits are situational. Observe what responses trigger particular reactions from other people, both negative and positive. When someone does X, should you do Y or Z? When *you* talk about A, do people react like B or C? What kinds of jokes are told to include people?

Take particular notice of how to create an upward spiral of amazing feelings and goodwill about you. <u>That's</u> social fluency.

Become the person that lights up a room and absolutely owns a conversation in an instantly likeable way… you <u>can</u> become that person. No one is born with these skills innately, and they were all learned to some degree. Just because they focused on some patterns that you didn't immediately catch doesn't mean you can't catch up to them now!

It's not an overnight process, but committing fully will shorten your learning curve substantially.

Monkey see, monkey do. Go get your bananas.

2. Overcoming your social fears and excuses.

Social fluency starts with leaving your room, opening your front door, and just going outside.

But that's not always the easiest process, is it?

It's not that deep down we wouldn't like to be able to overcome our insecurities and fears and just go out and talk to people. Maybe even talk to that hottie across from you at the bar and ask them out on a date?

But life gets in the way sometimes. You're not feeling it that night. You have an early day at work tomorrow and you need to get a full night's rest. You don't think you'll have fun at that party. That person isn't even that cute, certainly not enough for you to talk to. You need to wash your hair.

Oh, really?

Those are all the **excuses** that we give ourselves to not have to confront our fears for another day. To avoid facing the social situations that will give us exposure to the patterns we need to learn social fluency!

Apply this approach to everything else in life and it's just unacceptable — afraid of the job assignment? You can't just avoid it.

You can't constantly run away from things that make you uncomfortable in life. Given how much in life makes us uncomfortable and pushes our comfort zones, that allows fear to rule *large* aspects of your life. It can be debilitating and the opposite of empowering.

The good news is that you don't have to see a psychiatrist to break free of these patterns. I've got 2 simple steps for you start confronting your fears and getting into the social situations that will help your growth.

First, pay attention to yourself.

Learn to recognize when you're operating out of fear, social or otherwise. Ask yourself if the reasons you're giving for not doing something are legitimate... only you can truly know.

Whenever you hear yourself say certain internal excuses or go into an internal monologue, pay attention to the following: "I'm just not a social person," "I don't have the time," "I'll get around to it when I have the time..."

They're basically aimed at preventing you from staring your fear in the eyes and actually going through with it. The best way to overcome the almost automatic fear chain reaction that you go through is to focus on the worst case scenario, which brings us to step 2.

Second, think about the realistic consequences.

They aren't that bad. Even the worst case scenario. If you say something awkward or make an off-color joke, so what? 2 seconds of confused conversation silence? Big deal.

You've pushed your comfort zones, and now can calibrate from that experience. The world won't end, the sun will still rise, and tomorrow you'll be so much better for pushing your comfort zone.

Let's say you go out to a bar and summon up the courage to talk to the hottie at the bar. You try to start a conversation and they flat out reject you. What's the real downside here?

Are you going to see that person again? Is your rejection televised for the whole world to see? Did the people around you record a video and upload it to YouTube?

Of course not!

The truth is you get rejected all the time. Small failures happen every day. You apply for credit, you don't always get accepted. You apply for a job, you don't always get accepted.

But do people fall apart when these things happen? Of course not. So look at it from that perspective. Ask yourself how bad can it get. What's the real damage?

By constantly magnifying the fear of rejection and viewing it as some sort of personal judgment against you, you fuel your fear instead of overcoming your fear and becoming a stronger person.

Rejection in a social setting doesn't mean that you're a bad person or that you're a less valuable person.

If you don't even leave the house, you don't even give yourself the opportunity for any positive gain.

If that process wasn't convincing enough, just think about the high costs you're paying when you give into your social fears. You're cutting off any chance you have at creating meaningful relationships and even meeting your life mate. You might be losing out on truly lucrative career opportunities and the promotions that you know you deserve.

The walls of your comfort zone become invisible prison walls, and that's no way to live.

When you read literature and you study history, who are our heroes? Who are the people who stand up head and shoulders against the sea of humanity? People who looked their fears in the eye and overcame them.

You might not be the next Winston Churchill or the next Napoleon, but that's not to say that you don't have your own personal giants to slay.

Nobody else will do it for you, so take that leap of faith today.

3. Social body over mind.

Clubs are notoriously difficult and uncomfortable environments for most people. It's loud, people are stumbling around drunk, and you can't hope to have any kind of conversation there. (Or maybe I'm just not 21 years old anymore...)

Yet we all have friends that love club-hopping and seem to thrive in that environment. Hell, you can probably throw them into any kind of social situation, and they'll instantly adjust their fluency to fit in perfectly each time.

I'd bet the house that if you asked this person what their secret is, they'd tell you that it's a conscious choice and mindset they make to be social.

It's not something that's always on. It's not something that is in effect by default. It's something that they consciously choose. And they can turn it on and off whenever they want.

How?

When you choose to physically act in a socially fluent manner, your mind will follow your decision.

Your external physical actions will inform your mental state of mind.

It's the phenomenon of the attribution theory that is so well studied in human psychology. By simply going through the physical motions of something, your mind will mentally note that you are okay with it... and when you accomplish a social victory, it will mentally note that you excel at it. And that's how confidence grows.

So focusing on simply **acting**, regardless of your fears, will trigger internal changes over a short period of time to enhance your social fluency.

All we can control as humans are our actions and reactions. You might have a lot of doubt and conflict about your fears, but if you resolve to just go through the motions and process, the results you see externally will translate to your mindset and confidence.

Now that we've established that external action is a necessary precursor for the internal changes... what are the external actions we should master to effect that improvement?

Just stand up straight.

When you look into any social setting or crowd, you will notice that there are certain people that carry themselves a certain way… and it's easy to spot them because of their powerful and confident posture. They're standing at attention with their arms loose at their sides in a position of power.

Don't shrink down into yourself and hunch your shoulders, while retracting your chest. We all know that's a universal signal for discomfort and anxiety.

Put your chin up, puff your chest out, and hold your arms behind you. This is going to feel unnatural and like you're showing off your cleavage at first, but take a look in the mirror and look at how much better you look instantly just by standing up straight.

Deep down those people that stand out in crowds – they might be amazingly unconfident or insecure. But guess what? We can't tell, and we treat them like how we perceive them physically.

When you assume powerful body language, you speak more loudly and project better. Exaggerate your facial expressions. Use bigger and more powerful gestures. Smile confidently and engage others. These are the hallmarks of acting socially fluent, and your mind will believe the physical reality that you've created for yourself.

This might be the most empowering proposition in this book, and that's saying a lot.

If you feel defeated or small inside, you can simply physically project the opposite and *change your reality*. Studies have shown that simply smiling more can improve people's moods exponentially, so imagine how just making the choice to act can help you.

At the most basic levels, **our brains are slaves to our bodies**. This is why so many of our daily decisions defy logic and can even be detrimental for us. However, we can bend it to our advantage in gaining social fluency by forcing the mind to accept certain realities that we physically project for ourselves.

It doesn't happen overnight, but it will happen. The more you go through the motions of social fluency and make the choice to do it, the more you can achieve and alter your internal mental state.

You might not even realize that it's happening until you're suddenly at a party socializing without a care in the world and think "I would not have been able to do this a month ago...!"

The more you practice, the better you get at it, and the better you will be able to feel about yourself **on command**.

4. Familiarity breeds social comfort.

The first time I gave a big talk, I was a teenager and anxious as hell.

The auditorium was somewhere I had never been before, I couldn't find the bathroom beforehand, and I got lost on the way there.

I always think back to that day and imagine how I would have improved the performance. The answer is crystal clear.

Just as the chapter title says, *familiarity breeds social comfort*. When you know the situation, location, and overall setting of an upcoming social situation, it's inevitable that you'll be exponentially more comfortable and socially fluent as a result of **increased predictability**.

So what could I have done specifically to help my speech?

I should have gone to the optional sound check so I wouldn't have had to fumble around with the microphone, the podium, and hearing my voice reverberate off the walls of that big auditorium.

I should have made sure that my driving directions were spot on and that there would be parking. I should have checked out the venue and taken notice of where the bathrooms were, where I was going to be waiting backstage, and where my friends and parents were going to be sitting.

So much of social fluency, and indeed social skills at large, depend on thinking quickly on your feet and sometimes pulling things out of thin air. It's not always easy, can be hit or miss, and reminds one of improv comedy.

If you're going to give a speech somewhere you haven't given a speech before, it can be a very stressful situation. This is especially true when you feel that you're not really a good speaker, or public speaking scares you.

But if you can *eliminate a source of social anxiety* right off the bat by preparing and familiarizing yourself beforehand, that's just the smart and optimal way to be socially fluent.

It takes the worry out of any elements that you are unfamiliar with, and makes things mostly predictable and within your control. This allows you to focus all of your efforts and mental bandwidth on the task at home, whether it's a tough speech or simply making new friends.

The more familiar you are, the more comfortable you get.

There's a deeper element to familiarity as well.

When you are taking a run-through of your social situation, take notice of the emotional state that you are in. There's no pressure, no anxiety, and you feel only excitement and confidence at the upcoming social situation. You're calm and comfortable.

Remember that feeling when you're about to enter the fray and think back to that **emotional anchor**. You can always have this emotional haven that you can reference and you can draw strength from.

This whole chapter is to explain a simple truth that everyone has definitely felt before in their lives.

You've probably got your normal neighborhood hangouts that you patronize frequently. You know who the players are, the staff recognizes you, you know the management practices, and that one trick to opening the bathroom door.

You feel like a king there because you are an insider and know the place inside and out. You're super comfortable talking to new people there, because you feel like you have the upper hand and that they are outsiders.

Why not try to emulate this feeling in every setting that you are in? It's hard to feel intimidated and lack social fluency when you're in your *proverbial backyard*.

Draw confidence from your familiarity, and let that confidence be reflected in your approach to people. You'll see how easy it is to begin a conversation, be likeable, work a room... and the more you do it, the more you'll be able to flex your social muscles.

5. Turn social fluency on like a light switch.

I don't care how shy you think you are, or how much of a social leper you view yourself as.

There has been at least one time in your life when you feel comfortable and happy being at the center of attention, and where you can make friends with anyone. When you've been in *the zone*.

This chapter is going to walk you through the process of identifying your most social states and how you can turn it on at a moment's notice.

First, we have to remember that your shyness/anxiety/nervousness is only a state of mind... and **states of mind can be consciously and willfully changed** in many ways.

When you dig deep, you'll find that there are certain aspects of your personality that are actually quite social. It's just waiting beneath negativity and anxiety of ""I just don't like small talk," or "I'm just not a social person at parties!" to be summoned and expressed.

The first step in turning on your social self at a moment's notice is to identify the range of your social states. Think about the last time you were pumped up and really in the zone. Now break that emotional state down. What made you feel that way, what was happening, and most importantly, why did you feel that way? Sketch out their broad outlines. Be completely honest with yourself. Get in touch with that emotional state.

What were the external triggers? Did something happen that pushed you into that social state? Was it a word that somebody said? Were you wearing certain clothes that helped you feel really comfortable in your skin? Did you go out with a specific friend?

What aspect of your psychology was fed by these triggers? Was it your need to be appreciated? Was it your need to be validated? Was it your need to conquer or to explore? Identify these and be clear regarding these emotional bases.

The second step in calling up your social self at a moment's notice is to pair physical rituals with the emotional triggers that you isolated earlier.

Certain emotional states can be called up based on our physical state, especially when they are paired together. As we've discussed, the body has 100% influence over the mind and what the mind perceives... so you literally make emotional connections between things that are happening physically with what you are feeling at the current moment.

Just think of it as a modern re-imagining of Pavlov's dog. Pavlov's dog began salivating every meal time, which was accompanied by a ringing bell. Eventually, the dog began to salivate at the sound of any bell because he was conditioned to believe that a bell means that food is coming.

Likewise, you can use an external stimuli call up mental states.

Visualize the emotional triggers that caused your moods, or surround yourself with the external triggers. Perform physical acts like push-ups, jumping up and down, slapping your wrists, breathing deeply, standing on the balls of our feet... anything small and subtle will do. And just like Pavlov's dog, eventually even if the triggers aren't present, you can literally train yourself to get into your desired social state.

After all, what good is having a social side if you can never let it surface?

The reason this is works is that you mimic your physical responses when you're at a peak social state.

Remember when you were talking to that highly attractive person of the opposite sex, your blood was probably flowing, your adrenaline was pumping...You can replicate that physical state by doing push-ups.

So when you do the push-ups, you can replicate the emotional state as well. That's what pushes you to a social state. The best part is that you can call it up whenever you want.

You can exert a high degree of mastery over your emotional state.

As the old saying goes, "The person who masters himself masters the world."

6. The buddy system isn't just for swimming.

People tend to be private about their insecurities and humiliations. It's a sad fact of life because it indicates that people aren't comfortable showing vulnerability.

Unfortunately, people that don't let others in on their fears are selling themselves seriously short when it comes to the potential of their growth. If you want to grow your social fluency and overcome any social anxiety you might possess, you need to let someone else in!

Release your fear of judgment and let someone know what you are anxious about, worried about, and want to accomplish but are too afraid of saying out loud. Tell them what your excuses are for not putting yourself out there socially, and let them be your support column. It will be a huge burden off your shoulders.

Wouldn't it be nice to have someone help you overcome the mental blocks and fears you have and help you reach your full social potential?

The main message here is to **seek out a social accountability buddy**.

Accountability buddies aren't a new concept – they are simply people that know your circumstances, check in with you, and keep you on track. Personal trainers and life coaches are probably the most popular example of an accountability buddy, as you are literally forced by them to get into shape and keep forward progress to your goals. *Social* accountability buddies are the same except for social growth and goals.

Accountability buddies keep you honest when you aren't honest with yourself, and can ultimately push you over your challenges to new heights.

Sometimes, their biggest value is simply in keeping you from *running away*. We've gone over this earlier in the book, but I can never repeat this enough. There are always a million reasons to not do something, and **very few** are usually valid. If you have an accountability buddy, they aren't going to accept your excuses and reasons.

They'll push you to face your challenges… because that's what is necessary to improve any trait. You need to live through those awkward social moments to become a better person.

They'll force you to face the old saying, "No pain, no gain!"

Because they sometimes have to take a hard stance against your momentary happiness, accountability buddies work best when they aren't your close friends or relatives... unless you've got some cold-hearted friends! They simply have to understand that any emotional distress you're feeling is only in passing, is helpful for your personal growth that you need to experience, and sympathy for you has to take the backseat.

In other words, this person will understand full well that you need to go through a certain degree of pain and discomfort for you to change. They will push you back and really force you to do what you need to do.

Your accountability buddy's job is to push you out of your comfort zone and keep pushing forward so you can experience the progress that you need to improve.

Of course, they won't just push you off the plank to drown if you aren't ready. They'll jump right behind you into the deep end, and you can draw strength from their support and presence in your goals.

The reality is that an accountability buddy makes you grow up. They don't allow you to cop out. They don't allow you to give yourself excuses.

The best part of it all is that you're both keeping *each other* in check. Because as much as your accountability partner helps you with your issues, you're also helping him or her with his or her own issues as well.

You grow together.

7. The barista is your guinea pig.

People are inherently self-absorbed.

I don't mean this in a negative sense. People just prioritize themselves and get caught in the busyness of their own lives. This makes finding people to help brush up your social fluency difficult.

Or does it?

Luckily, there is one segment of society that is especially suited to help you practice your social skills. In fact, they don't really have much of a choice. I'm referring *to service people*.

Baristas. Cab drivers. Cashiers. The grocery bag boy. Waiters. Doormen. Valets.

Why are they so suited to practicing social skills with?

First of all, they are quite literally paid to be nice to you.

Their job performance depends on their customer service skills, and if they want to keep their jobs, they have to be courteous to you.

This alone should eliminate the fear you have of crashing and burning in any social interaction, because it's their job to prevent that and probably laugh at your jokes. You'll see that crashing and burning is never really that bad, and people move on quickly.

Second of all, they don't any choice!

They're a captive audience behind the counter or cash register. They are usually stuck being stationary in a position for long periods of time, and for those who have held the above jobs… you know that it's not the most thrilling life. Most of the time, they are bored out of their minds, so having someone engage them will be a positive experience for them. You will make their day pass faster and just give them something to do.

You might be the only one to treat them with respect and show actual interest in them as a person, which would undoubtedly make you the highlight of their day. In other words, they'll be glad to talk to you.

So now that we know WHY service people are great to practice with… what benefits do you actually get by doing so? It's pretty simple, actually.

You get unlimited shots at the goal.

If you're out at a bar or networking event, you only have one shot at making the right impression. If you fall flat on your face, as will inevitably happen from time to time, guess what? That was your one shot at the goal and you need to find someone else to practice with.

With service people, you can test different stories, reactions, phrases, greetings, facial expressions, and so on. Unless you offend them in a deeply personal way, they'll still be courteous to you, but you can gauge how positive their reactions are to all of your behaviors to know what works best. You can continuously improve and hone your skills. You can see your progress with future interactions. As you see their reactions change, you can fine-tune what you're doing and keep stepping up your game.

Essentially, you're in a *safe environment to practice and polish your social skills* without fear of any judgment or consequences. More than that, you can learn to read people, process their signals, and calibrate your interactions to different types of people.

This is a process that takes trial and error, but you can speed it up exponentially by engaging with service people.

8. Storytelling as influencing.

Studies have shown that more people can name the characters on the television show The Brady Bunch than the Ten Commandments.

Surprisingly and random? Yes.

But it shows in a very salient way that people respond to stories and narratives far better than lists and sets of rules.

Throughout your life, you've met many different interesting people... but you don't remember all of them. Not even close. You remember those who could entrance you with a story, or had colorful stories about their own lives.

If you want to increase your charisma and influence, undoubtedly large factors of social fluency, mastering the art of telling great stories is paramount.

Amazing stories boost your social fluency because stories radiate comfort. When you're weaving your story, you feel comfortable because you're taking the lead and sharing your experiences with them – there is no fear of judgment because the story itself doesn't reflect on you and you don't feel threatened.

Most importantly, you're drawing your listeners into an emotional world where you control exactly what emotions are felt, and how strong they are. And they have no choice but to go along with it. It's also comforting for them because they don't have to put in any work while you're telling a story, so it's a situation that complete control is essentially handed to you. They're putting their faith in you at that moment to dictate the interaction.

That's the very definition of influence.

You don't have influence over someone who's emotions you can't dictate. You don't have influence over someone who isn't comfortable around you. You don't have influence over someone who feels threatened by you. You don't have influence outside of situations where control is readily given.

When you tell a story, all of these evaporate, and you draw people into your zone of influence.

So how do we tell better stories?

First, we should focus on which emotions we want to convey and why people should care about them. As educated, intellectual, academic, and logical as people might seem, deep down we are all emotional animals.

We all bleed. We all feel fear. We all want love. We all want to feel appreciated. We all want to be accepted. We all want to feel that we belong.

We have all these common wants and needs. These are the raw ingredients that a master storyteller works with. By establishing familiarity and rapport with these common baseline needs and emotions, we are able to dissolve the wall between us and other people.

A great storyteller communicates that "I am you" and "You are me," that there is really nothing separating us. And once you get that person to that emotional level, you can go in any direction you wish with them.

This is why dictators are such effective speakers. This is why certain speakers are able to capture the popular imagination. They are great storytellers, and the foundation of any great story is an emotional bedrock of commonality.

Is there any some sort of template to better stories? Are there patterns to follow to become a better storyteller?

Actually, there are. Whether you're looking at the Bible, or you're looking at King Arthur's Round Table, or Ancient Greek Mythology, they all fit certain patterns.

In fact, even Shakespeare's plays fit certain narrative patterns. By paying attention to these patterns, you can then copy them in how you tell your story.

There are really three basic story types, and you can basically massage all sorts of stories based on these story types.

These are the hero cycle, the adventure cycle, and the story arc. By paying attention to how these work, you can make any personal story engaging, and most importantly, emotionally truthful.

9. Act familiar, become familiar.

The best salespeople you don't even realize are selling you until you end up with an armload of knick knacks that you have absolutely zero need for.

They'll sidle up to you, pretend to browse whatever you're currently looking at, and start asking questions that aren't particularly sales-y in nature. They'll build rapport, find out what shared interests you have in common, and bond over things completely unrelated to whatever they are selling.

They just act like your friends... and who do you trust, if not your friends? Fast forward to your armload of robot toy dogs.

This demonstrates *the power of mirroring*.

In many ways, human psychology is exceedingly simple. We don't usually like the unfamiliar, and we do like those who think like us and are similar to us.

People that navigate the world in the same way that we do, and have the same interests and beliefs. The socially fluent know this, and actively seek to appear similar to others to dissolve the walls of separation that people might hold up.

When those walls come down, trust and emotional openness are possible. There are also a few beneficial assumptions we make about people that seem to be similar to us.

The first assumption is that they are on your level status-wise, however you define the word. This is a powerful psychological component in being interested and curious in what someone has to say. If you feel that someone is the same status as you, or even slightly higher, you're simply going to want to make a good impression on them and connect more. This bodes well for any conversation.

The second assumption is that you are both privy to exclusive knowledge and experiences. The two of you inhabit a world that no one else knows about, so a strong bond is immediately created on the basis of sharing that specialized knowledge or experience. And just as with the first assumption, there is a psychological effect that is created that makes opening up and connecting all the easier.

The third and final assumption is that besides status, you are simply similar to them as a whole. People like people like themselves, it's a simple fact. People will also seek out others like themselves, be more likely to help others like themselves, and seek to integrate them into their friend circles. Don't we bond immediately with people from our same hometown or school?

It's not like you're trying to manipulate people, it's not like you're trying to fool people or lie to people. Instead, you're using the power of mirroring to get that same emotional state with others.

Regardless of what the person looks like, or what college or university that person went to, or what that person does for a living, it doesn't matter. You will have certain traits that you will share with that person.

We're all human beings and deep down, we're not all that different from each other. Find that area that you have in common.

Think of it this way: *when you act like a friend, you will be treated like one very quickly*. Alternatively, if you act like an enemy, you will be treated like one very quickly.

Once you get that person, at least on an emotional level, to stop looking at you as a threat or as a stranger, then you can become more comfortable. And the more comfortable you become, the more comfortable he or she becomes.

The socially fluent look at the prospect, study the prospect for a few seconds, assume familiarity with how that person conducts himself or herself, and then starts mirroring.

But really, let's bring it all back to the title of this chapter: *act familiar, become familiar*. People will gravitate to those they see themselves in a little bit, so act instantly comfortable as a friend would... and seize upon the commonalities you share to cement the bond.

10. Understand and take advantage of conversation patterns.

Let's face it, most conversations in our daily lives begin and end in the same, mundane way.

"Hey, how's it going?"

"Good, you?"

"Same! Talk to you later!"

This is perfectly acceptable... if you want to be described as mundane yourself, but that's not what we're going for in this book.

If you want to produce better outcomes from your social interactions, understanding how most conversations progress is key. It turns out that most follow certain patterns, as most actions beget a similar reaction. You can predict this, shape and control it, and turn it to your advantage by directing it.

Seizing control of your social interactions is a pretty powerful concept.

The first pattern you must learn to recognize is that most conversations begin and end the same way. I'm willing to bet that you've repeated the script above at least once today if you've left your home.

People, myself included, follow certain scripts and templates for a few reasons.

First, it's what social courtesy dictates of us. We are polite to people on a surface level on a daily basis, so we must at a minimum acknowledge people and politely ask how they are.

Second, the social situations we find ourselves in on a daily basis aren't very unique. It might be with a co-worker, someone on a bus, or a friend, but these aren't situations that warrant any more thought than using a script or template. It's not every day that we basejump from the Empire State Building.

Finally, people aren't that creative on a daily basis. It's too much effort to come up with an original way to begin and end each interaction, so they stick with what's lazy and tried and true.

Once we understand this pattern, we can better prepare for how to make ourselves stand out and channel social fluency, namely by leading the interaction from the outset.

Knowing that people stick to their conversation scripts and templates out of laziness or social courtesy, this means that there is a massive opportunity for you to take the lead of a conversation, both subject and tone-wise.

Remember, most people have a lazy approach to interactions, so they are *completely open* to your taking the lead… because that is less effort for them.

So think back to the last few conversations you've had, and you'll notice that they are basically triggered by the same body of questions. Separate those questions down into categories, and you'll see that there is a limited range of categories that people stick to that you can prepare for easily.

Your state of well-being. Your weekend. Your family. Last night. Work. Your significant other. Your hobbies. The weather. Shared people, experiences, and circumstances.

By developing more in-depth questions and answers to these basic question types, you can find yourself leading every conversation in the direction that you want while appearing amazingly intuitive and socially fluent.

For the simple yes and no questions people give you, provide in-depth answers with details, mini stories, and humor.

For the simple yes and no answers people give you, ask them probing, open-ended questions about their lives and circumstances.

Instead of conversations dependent on simple yes and no answers and questions, you can inject massive amounts of personality and create a conversation with actual depth.

Make sure that your body language is congruent with someone that is engaged, interested, and committed to having an in-depth conversation. Stand up straight, lean forward, physically show that you are engaged and attentive, and give them great reactions to their answers to your questions. Don't cross your arms, lean back, or scan the rest of the room with your eyes.

Your body language plays a huge role in how people receptive people will be to your taking lead of the interaction, and how your message and tone will be received.

Finally, lead by injecting positive energy, passion, and conviction into your conversations. You can create the social outcomes you want by radiating the kind of energy to the other person that you want back.

I can't say this enough: *humans are emotional creatures*.

When you radiate positive energy and passion, it excites the recipient. The conversation, instead of becoming boring and dead, actually becomes exciting, passionate, and mutually gratifying.

11. Conversations as pure entertainment.

Just as the vast majority of conversations fall prey to certain scripts and templates that people use out of laziness or convention… most conversations are also boring and extremely forgettable.

There are only so many ways people communicate with each other on a regular basis.

Again, this is fine if your goal is to blend in and not make an impression on the people that you meet.

But if you're trying to convey social fluency, generate a sale, or flirt up a storm with the opposite sex… it goes without saying that your conversations probably should not be boring. It just screams low value, and can lead to the other person viewing you as not worth doing business with, flirting with, or even just engaging with.

In other words, boring is death. The purpose of conversations are many, but *if they are entertaining to both parties, they can transcend barriers.* Therefore, make that your singular goal.

If you want to achieve more success with your social life and professional life, you have to find a solution to boring conversations. Sometimes they become exciting and interesting organically, but there are certain tricks and mindsets you can use to spice up conversations in your daily life.

First, if you're in a boring conversation, it's because you have also let it become boring.

You have the full power to control of a conversation and make it as entertaining or probing as you want. So seize control and <u>don't rely on others to entertain you</u>. Embody the mindset that you possess the power to change your circumstances in a snap.

Second, understand that everyone possesses a quirky and fun side.

Everyone is abnormal on some level, and this is what makes them beautiful. It's our weirdness and odd thought patterns that give us our identity. More importantly, it's what gives people personality and the fodder for some interesting conversation material.

So don't be afraid to share your own quirky or nonconventional view on a subject. This strays from the norm and will make people react in ways that break their scripts and templates. Go out on a limb, take a stance, and show conviction. It will also encourage them to share their own unique views on subjects, and suddenly you're in a real, substantive, and entertaining conversation!

When you mirror each other's unusual takes on a particular subject, you're basically being emotionally open with each other. Instead of walling off each other and condemning each other as unusual, this opens an opportunity for bonding.

"You know what? We're not so different, you and I. I have that side to me too!"

The way people actually connect with others and enjoy their company is because of their idiosyncrasies. You don't become friends with someone because they meet your ideals or standards. **You just find each other amusing and entertaining, and that's the entire basis of friendship at the outset**.

Third, just keep conversations light and amusing. Make it about entertainment value.

Don't start with a soliloquy about your mother's irritable bowel syndrome. There is a time and place for deep conversations about emotional wounds and healing, but they are far and few inbetween.

The vast majority of daily conversations will benefit greatly from just viewing them as an opportunity to joke around with someone, instead of engaging with them to gain something. Grow the mindset of interacting with people and things in your daily life just to see what happens when you poke them, and it will serve you well in conversations.

Work on not filtering your thoughts as much. See what reactions you can provoke. Ask ridiculous hypotheticals. Seek to find the humor in any situation. Ask what hilarious situations something you see reminds you of. Compare an innocent bystander to a Disney character. Answer questions with movie references. Think out loud.

Finally, don't be afraid to "go there."

Don't be afraid to jump into so-called taboo topics, because 99.99% of the time, people are completely fine with topics that others would call offensive, improper, or rude.

Taboo topics are often more personal in nature, so in addition to creating an interesting line of conversation, you've just made it infinitely more personal and deep. You've connected substantively, while engaging people more.

Most people are busy trying to be safe and stay polite. That approach is actually yawn-inducing and boring, and probably reflects their approach in other aspects of life. They're filtering themselves to a fault and not showing their true selves.

If you act like everyone else, don't expect to make an impression.

12. Be unapologetically you.

In my capacity as a social skills coach, I see a lot of people struggle with the same humps and bumps.

One of the most important humps that I help people overcome is their need to try to appeal to everyone socially – essentially being a *people pleaser* and being friends with everyone.

If this is your personal philosophy, odds are that you aren't happy and comfortable enough with yourself to have the confidence that people will accept you for who you really are... and you might never be truly happy because you'll be constantly seeking validation and approval from others.

Unfortunately, this thinking highly affects how we relate and interact with each other. **People feel that they have to say certain things and act a certain way to be accepted and appreciated.**

The truth is that if you try to please everyone, you will become amazingly forgettable. Lukewarm. Blank. Just "nice."

You'll at best connect on an "adequate friend" level with everyone, and that's not a title that I consider favorable or impressive. Additionally, the "adequate friend" connections you make will rarely turn into real friendships, and instead remain stuck in acquaintance mode.

Instead, live with integrity to your true, unapologetic self. You may not reach the "adequate friend" level of connection with everyone, but you allow yourself the possibility for "new best friend" connections, with scattered "we will never talk again" connections. You may be slightly polarizing, but the reality is in any type of social setting, you're bound to turn off certain people. That means others are bound to love who you truly are and why wouldn't you want to surround yourself with those people?

Even if you end up alienating 90% of the people you come across... why surround yourself with those who don't like your true self? What end does that serve? Why hang around others if they don't really like you, and you have to become a sanitized or false version of yourself to fit in with them?

If you can live with and embrace this fact, you're halfway there to being comfortable in your own skin.

When people look at you, they get what they see. You never say things you don't mean, you don't lie to people, you don't put on an act, you don't do things to impress people... you don't do any of that.

One way to look at it is to *play to win* in terms of making real friends.

By being unapologetically you, you filter for your real friends. Real friends will love you and accept you for who you are, not because of somebody you pretend to be. Real friends know that you love what you love and you hate what you hate, and either agree or accept it readily. Real friends appreciate you for who you are, warts and all. These are people who look at your weaknesses and fall in love with you.

Don't just play the friendship game to mitigate losses in terms of making friends by being a generically nice version of yourself to everyone. By playing a percentage game and putting on an act so you can make the most friends, you lose touch of who you really are and will eventually gain a wide circle of mere acquaintances. That's no way to go through life.

Personal authenticity is the key to acceptance by others and a well-lived life. If you're not authentic with yourself, you really can't be authentic with other people.

Don't try to always impress other people. Don't try to put on a show. Don't put others on a pedestal. Who cares what they want?

Focus on what's important to you, project that, and find your tribe instantly.

13. Figure out your social triggers.

One of the greatest findings in the past years of human psychology is the realization that many of our mental processes are incredibly subconscious.

We think we know why we react the way we do in social situations, and why we like certain people.

But we're not always correct because the conscious brain only sees a few pieces of the overall puzzle. When we see circumstances in our lives, we try to rationalize it, make excuses for it, and otherwise twist our sense of logic to fit what we see… **often inaccurately**.

This is occasionally a frightening thought, but most of the time we can and should be able to take advantage of it.

It means that you have subconscious triggers to put you into your most social moods… it just requires a bit of self-analysis and introspection to find them.

We all have friends and circumstances where we feel like we're the kings and queens of the moment. Maybe you've got that one friend who brings out your charming and hilarious side, or maybe you're the main entertainer at any family function.

What is it about those interactions that subconsciously launches us into our best behaviors and habits? What social and emotional triggers get us in the zone of social fluency?

As long as you are aware of the triggers that push you to respond to certain situations in a certain way, you can manipulate these triggers to work for your benefit.

This is doubly true with social situations – certain types of people, moods, locations, and even weather can bring out the awkward and socially inept in us, or the charming and magnetic.

So what triggers bring out the best, the worst, and the funny side to you? Find the triggers that produce positive responses and moods, and you can summon them at any time without having to be in the presence of that trigger.

People are strong triggers.

There are certain friends who interact with you in such a way that your funny and magnetic sides come out. In fact, you can be the most charming person in the room when you surround yourself with these people.

Study how these friends bring out your best side. Identify their manner of interaction with you, and how you play off of them. Was it a word? Was it a look? Was it some form of mannerism? Was it how they react to you? Is it how they egg you on?

When you can understand and isolate these external triggers, you become your best self in any situation by extreme visualization techniques.

Say you have a friend named **Rudy** that you are just hilarious around. You've isolated that it's because he has a dry, sarcastic sense of humor that you play well off of, and can always add to.

Obviously, you can't have Rudy around you at all times to help you in social situations. But you now know that you do very well with sarcasm – sarcasm is one of your social triggers. So when you are in social situations, *visualize Rudy's sarcasm* contributing to the conversation in the background, and it will summon your inner Chris Rock.

That's how you can turn on your social side at will, by simply identifying your triggers. Just like with most things in your personal emotional life, awareness is half the battle. You'll find that anything can be a trigger for you, not just people. It's a powerful awareness that eliminates all excuses you have about your social reservations.

When you are fully aware of how certain mental pictures trigger certain emotional reactions, you can then make substitutions for these visualizations, based on your own decisions, based on your own choosing.

That's how you take full control and full ownership of how you perform in a wide range of social settings. Truly social people know how this works. This is why they can always be at their best regardless of external circumstances.

Zero in on certain visualizations to trigger a social state, and seize control of your best self.

14. What you say doesn't really matter.

Having people like you has **nothing** to do with what you say.

Repeat.

It does not matter what you say.

One of the biggest problems with most social and conversation skills books is that they place focus on the *entirely wrong aspects of interaction*. They focus on the words coming out of your mouth, what you should say, or how to avoid silences.

But think about it from this perspective – does *any* of that stuff matter if you like the person and have great conversation chemistry and energy with them? Does it matter if they say something odd, or there's an occasional silence here and there? Can't you talk about your bowel movements with your great friends and have a great time?

So the chapter title is a bit sensationalist, but my point remains that people are more attracted by how you say things than what you say, because that is what leads to conversational chemistry and actual friendship.

If connecting with people was based purely on saying the right thing, social fluency would just be too easy, wouldn't it? There would be books full of the correct phrases to use in each situation and in response to each question… and just by plugging them in, you would be able to gain friends in a snap. Obviously, no such book exists because the notion is absurd.

It's just not how human psychology works.

People are attracted to you because of *how* you say things because that's what really reflects your character. People are always instinctually trying to read you, and your delivery, tone, accompanying gestures, and facial expressions give them clues to judge you accurately. Conversational chemistry is created by how people take to your character and want to connect with you, not just because you've said the right joke at the right time.

People are more drawn by energy and chemistry than content.

We're drawn by how fun people seem to be based on the chemistry that's present when they talk to us. We are drawn by how passionate they are regarding the things that they're talking about. We may not agree with what they're saying, but the level of passion and interest regarding the things that they're talking about definitely give us clues as to what's important to them, and how they are as people.

People don't really ever get the chance to tell you what they're about, or just what kind of people they are, so we learn to infer these things from the tone and manner in which they communicate. It might even take time for those things to come to light, or only come through shared experiences. And unfortunately, people aren't going to fill out a questionnaire and say honestly that's who they are.

You have to figure out yourself by looking at these different signals and these different clues. One of the biggest clues people give off subconsciously is their level of passion and the amount of chemistry you have when you talk to them.

People feed off positive vibes. There's a common response process here that when people get motivated by your energy level, they reflect that back to you. When you feel it, your energy level goes up even more, and you reflect it back to them.

You end up building each other up, instead of dragging each other down. This leads to an emotional bond that is the basis of great friendships.

When you're that person in the room who consistently sends off positive vibes, people will seek you out. You will instantly become the most popular person in the room.

When you are that person that gives off energy, people respond to it by reaching deep down inside and triggering their own capacity for positive emotions and positive passion, and this results in a response that lights up the room.

Eventually, there will be enough people in the room to radiate it back to make that positive emotional energy source a self-sustaining source.

15. Condition emotional attraction.

As much as we'd like to believe that we're driven by logic and reasoning, nine times out of ten our actions are actually due to impulse and emotional triggers whether we realize it or not.

Sometimes we can come up with a passable justification to explain our actions after the fact, but the fact still remains that if we're honest with ourselves, most of our actions come as emotional responses.

If we were to define ourselves purely with logic and reason, there would be no differentiating us and computers. Our world would be entirely predictable, and not in a positive sense.

Once you accept this reality, you will be able to take advantage of it with the power of conditioned emotional attraction.

Conditioned emotional attraction is a fancy term for a simple concept: when you act in a certain way that people enjoy being around and make people feel good, they will be attracted to you.

In other words, positivity gets positive responses, and imparting good feelings makes you magnetic.

We gravitate towards positive people because we want that feeling in our life. We want our own positive sides to come out, and know that positivity is inherently good for our mental well-being. Positivity just makes people feel good, and is the precursor to other great emotions such as love, attraction, friendship, and ecstasy.

Therefore, take advantage of conditioned emotional attraction by being the one to give out positive emotions and vibes. Send positive signals to people you speak to. Smile incessantly. Praise as opposed to criticize. Compliment as opposed to nitpick. Make laughter your default reaction as opposed to confused silence. Don't be negative and talk about political issues that will either bore or polarize people.

You can't necessarily control whether people will always like you, but you can control your impression to be positive and impart good feelings… which makes people want to be around you, plain and simple.

Of course, this operates in reverse as well. If you send out negative vibes – not laughing when people make jokes, not smiling, turning to buzzkill conversation topics, nitpicking on people's choice of words, or criticizing – you'll get a negative response back.

The problem is that negative responses from other people don't always come in the form of direct feedback… they just might not hang out with you anymore, so it's a bit harder to tell.

Conditioned emotional attraction is a choice, and you can either cultivate it in a positive or negative manner.

First, you need to make the choice to feel good yourself.

You're not going to be able to make others feel good if you don't yourself, and anything you attempt in the meantime will be transparent and fake. Put yourself in a positive mindset because… why not? Did you lose your both of your parents, your significant other, and your job in the past week? It could be worse!

Second, get personal.

Think about the person you're talking to, and how you can brighten up their day with your positivity. What do they pride themselves on, or what are they insecure about? Make it a point to emphasize those aspects. What compliment will do best with them? What kind of personality do they vibe best with? Are they a talker or a listener?

Remember, your goal is simply to make other people come away from interactions with you thinking "I may not be sure why, but I really enjoyed talking to him/her!"

The bottom line and main assertion I'm making here is that conditioned emotional attraction is very real. When people know that *interacting with you is going to be a positive experience that they will come away enjoying and never regretting...* well, they'll be seeking our your company more, won't they?

Remember that conversation isn't really about what's said. The important part that will increase your social fluency is to focus on the feelings that you create within people. This is how business deals get started, this is how friendships are formed, and this is how relationships are explored.

Everyone is constantly sending signals that determine whether or not we want to interact with them more – take the initiative to make sure that your signals are the porch light to people's moths.

16. Own group discussion dynamics.

Here's another question I get asked frequently that I want to address in a definitive fashion.

How do I talk to a group of people at large?

<u>You don't</u>.

When you address a group at large, you can engage on entirely shallow topics like the weather, but realize that it probably won't get deeper than that for numerous reasons. Spend your requisite time smiling and nodding at the edge of a circle of people talking.

The dynamics of addressing a group, a random collection of people that might not have anything in common, are extremely limiting.

The dynamics make group-wide speeches and topics pretty bland, because you can't get too personal— it will be invasive to broadcast someone's personal life in such detail with a whole group, and other people probably won't care about the mundanities of one person's life if they're not involved in it.

Talking in a group also means that you can't focus on one person, because everyone else will get bored if the conversation doesn't have anything to do with them.

Another problem with group discussion situations is that people are extremely tentative and never want to make the first move... because they don't want to read the group dynamic incorrectly and say the wrong thing.

For many people, a very real nightmare is to say something and have people give you a look of confusion and disgust... which is exponentially hellish in a group discussion. They are waiting for someone to take the lead and set the tone, and no one wants to do it incorrectly.

This means there are only a very limited amount of topics that you can discuss in groups, and they are by and large very boring and shallow. When we try to appeal to more than one person, only those shallow and general topics fit the bill in terms of making people feel included.

Yup, you'll be stuck talking about the surprisingly chilly weather or the deadly traffic for longer than you ever want if you don't learn to veer away from typical group discussion dynamics.

So what's the fix for this? As I said before, don't even try to address the group as a whole unless you feel like you can sustain the group's energy, and you have enough non-generic topics up your sleeve that will both appeal to that particular group. (I'll get into this later…)

Just start with your neighbors. Knowing what we know about group discussion dynamics, and what we are ultimately trying to accomplish by increasing our social fluency, it should be natural at this point for you to want to start with just one person and build a rapport and connection.

All chance of building a true connection is lost when a group converges on a singular topic, so your mission within a group is to make the best of friends with your neighbors. Engage them, be enthusiastic about their interests, ask them a lot of leading questions, be a great listener, give them the emotional reactions that they are seeking, and sustain positivity. Nothing new.

The only thing that you have to do differently when engaging your neighbors in a group discussion dynamic is to be slightly louder and exaggerate your reactions slightly more than you might otherwise.

This is because as your conversation with your neighbors becomes more and more in depth and interesting, you are going to attract the attention of the entire group eventually.

Being louder and exaggerating allows them to eavesdrop in a sense, but more importantly, it keeps them out of your conversation for longer because it gives the sense that you are both very intensely into it, which discourages interruption.

The more passionate a conversation between, the more invasive people feel interrupting it.

To recap: forget attempting to address the group as a whole unless you are uniquely situated with the group and its interests. Instead, focus on getting to know your neighbors in a non-shallow manner, and work on exaggerating and making your reactions a bit louder than they normally would be to prolong the discussion with your neighbors when the group's attention eventually turns to you.

A final thing to remember is that socially, people look to others to take the lead… not out of some need, but just out of not having to take the leap and possibly saying the wrong thing.

If you want to truly address a group all at once, you'll have to take the lead 100% and forego the neighbor-spiral technique I just described. You'll have to direct the group as a conductor directs an orchestra — by pointing to one group member to play a solo on their instrument, and making that intertwine with the rest of the group members and their solos.

If you've ever partaken in a book club or setting where there was a discussion leader, that's the role you'll have to embody.

Ask leading questions for the group, distill the answers, ask others what they think about it, and generally be the main hub through which all dialogue flows.

Sound tiring? It sure is, but can be worth it if it fits your personality. Instead of having group discussions stalled by lulls and buzzkill topics, you can expertly trigger a group member's reaction or thoughts and pick up the overall energy of the group time and time again.

Instead of having your group discussions ruined by peaks and valleys where there's a lot of dead space, you can play the role of the maestro and play the discussions based on the interests you perceive from the members of the group. If that conversation topic is beginning to wind down, you can trigger another member to talk about things that they're interested in, and this will pick up the overall energy level of the group.

This is not about you hogging the spotlight. This is not about you becoming a prima donna and being the source of all wisdom in the group. That's not the point. The whole point is to give everybody an equal chance to shine and share.

Best of all, you alone keep the genuine opportunities for interpersonal bonding alive between all group members.

When you're able to do this, then people are attracted to you because this is a key indicator of real interpersonal leadership.

17. Genuine social habits.

The power of habit is stronger than our willpower and discipline on a daily basis.

Sometimes these habits are positive, but more often than not they are negative, and borne out of emulating the wrong people or just sheer laziness.

And in social settings, poor social habits can be damaging and completely obscure the value and effect of what you're trying to actually impart.

Just imagine that you're on a date with someone, and they seem to subconsciously lick their lips whenever mention anything about sex. Regardless of whether you were going to attempt the act with them that date, their oddball habit might be too much of a turnoff to overcome.

Or say that someone seems adamantly opposed to eye contact, and keeps scanning the room behind you while you talk, making it seem like they haven't heard a word you said.

One of the biggest challenges people have with mastering social fluency is that they can't control their social habits, which means that the messages they want to communicate will seldom be congruent with what the other person perceives.

In other words, their non-verbal social habits can completely corrupt and disrupt the message they actually want to send. Your responsibility to social fluency does not end one you visualize the words that you are going to speak.

Once again, we find that the actual substance of what we say is far less important than the tone and feeling we convey to others.

The repeated emphasis here is on the realization that you can completely control all aspects of your social fluency if you gain awareness and put in the work. Your social habits are no exception. There's a lot we can do to counter those behavioral patterns so that more of our social interactions yield positive results.

How do you even define a negative social habit?

They trip you up. Make you more difficult to understand. Introduce misinterpretations. Overall, short-circuit your ability to communicate with people on a verbal and non-verbal level.

This simple definition makes it very easy to identify them, which is half the battle in self-improvement – awareness.

Does your speaking tone skew negative, and does it match up with the overall message that you're trying to convey? Is your sarcasm actually understandable, or are you coming off like an asshole?

Do you attempt to make eye contact? Do you stare too much, or do your eyes drift aimlessly when someone speaks?

Do you tend to use filler words or noises a lot when you speak to others? Does that convey your inner anxiety, or is it merely a crutch that has become habitual over the years?

Do you fidget with your hands, legs, or face when interacting with others? Does this convey the inner lack of confidence you might have, or do you simply have a lot of excess energy?

The above aren't necessarily habits for success, but it's important to conduct a self-awareness check on them because while you and I know that it may not mean that you're unconfident or horny, people will make their own judgments and perceptions that are usually unfair.

Negative social habits don't just impact your ability to communicate effectively, they induce a downward spiral that is very salient in how it affects your confidence and communication skills.

When you commit a negative social habit, you will get a reaction from your conversation partner that is lukewarm or negative. You will likely notice this reaction, and feel self-conscious about your social fluency… which in turn makes you more anxious and commit more negative social habits out of nerves. You will both reflect the emotional states that you've given each other, and the conversation is no longer something that represents positive feelings to either of you.

You must also resist the urge to judge your own behaviors negatively because that will just contribute to the downward spiral. Lack of confidence, self-conscious, frozen, afraid. Many things can affect your emotional states, but you should never be the one to put it down.

The solution is straightforward – take proactive control of your social habits.

Constantly be aware of the signals you're giving out. You have to remember that you have to be deliberate when you're talking to people. People are always sizing you up, people are trying to figure out who you are. The bottom line is they're trying to determine whether they can trust you.

By being aware of the signals you're sending out, you can put yourself in a position to correct your behavior in real time. This is very important because if you want to control or correct a behavior, you have to be aware of it first.

18. Take control of your feedback loops.

Just as our social habits comprise more of our message than the actual words coming out of our mouth, so do the social <u>behaviors</u> that we all engage in.

We just send out so many messages that it is impossible for verbal words to be any more than a small fraction of what we convey.

If you even just look tired, guess what? You're sending out a message that you might not really want to be talking to that person, and from there it's a slippery slope of what assumptions people will make. If you look excited you'll also get a certain reaction and assumption from others.

The reality is that how we choose to show our body language impacts the kind of reaction we get, and hence **we create our own social feedback loops**.

When we choose how we express ourselves, we choose the response that we get from the world. This is the social feedback loop that you can gain power over instantly, because it's a choice.

That is one of the most empowering things you can ever realize and it's a choice that you make on a daily basis.

Because instead of feeling that there's really not much you can do about it about the world, it lets you know that you can take full control over your life.

Unfortunately, most people go about life and interpersonal communications in a reactive way. We react instead of planning out our responses and messages.

Instead of responding to situations with other people based on our values and intentions, we're basically like instinctive animals that basically wait for external signals to happen, then we just automatically react. This is hardly a recipe for interpersonal success, or any other kind of success for that matter.

Just as we can ensure that our feedback loops are positive and uplifting, we can also fall prey to very common negative feedback loops.

Other people bounce back those negative signals to you. Once you perceive those negative signals, you feel discouraged, judged, diminished, and so on. So how do you react? You do what comes naturally: you bounce off even worse signals.

When others receive this, what do you think they will do? That's right: they will bounce off negative signals back, and then it goes on and on and on, and it proceeds in a downward spiral. Nobody wins. This is a negative feedback loop.

If you feel that your social world is a hostile place, or you feel misunderstood all the time, pay attention to the signals you were sending out. Chances are, there's a negative feedback loop there somewhere.

So how do you fix this?

Fix your externalities. These are things that people can see. Assume the right posture, send out the right body language, and make sure that you're in full control or at least in full awareness of your facial tics and expressions. For example, if you want to make people feel excited about your ideas, look excited. Don't look angry or sad or depressed or resigned.

The best way to do this of course is to be mindful of how you're talking and what your face looks like while you're expressing your ideas. If you look like a person who's on fire and is driven by passion for the amazing cutting-edge ideas he or she is talking about, that level of excitement is infectious to the person listening to you, and will be bounced back to you, and the communication can be a positive one.

However, even if you're talking about the best idea, the best thing since sliced bread, but you have your arms crossed, and you have your legs crossed, and you're leaning back, chances are the person in front of you is basically not going to be interested or defensive. The worst part of this is that you set yourself up to fail.

The key point here is that you're always in control.

You can always choose the outcome of your social interactions.

BONUS – The ONE exercise to instantly improve your social confidence.

Believe it or not, there's a simple exercise that you can do right now to instantly improve the confidence with which you approach all social situations. You can even do it while you're reading this book.

You've done it countless times before, even as a child. It's mindbogglingly easy and can be practiced every day in a couple of minutes. However, you might not have done it in years, and even if you had, you wouldn't have known what to focus on.

Ready?

Read out loud.

Just read 400 words out loud on a daily basis, and especially before you head to a social gathering or situation. Choose different passages each day and make sure to exaggerate emotions, dialogue, and reactions to the nth degree.

It turns out that most of us don't speak to people that much during the day, which ends up atrophying your social muscles and voice. So what can it do for you?

It will improve your vocal projection and strengthen your voice, making sure you are never meekly talking again.

It will improve your enunciation and reduce word stumbling, and make you a much more articulate speaker in general.

It will teach you how to breathe properly and how to pace your sentences and phrases for maximum impact of delivery.

It will help you learn how to accurately convey emotional highs and lows through changes in vocal inflection.

It will warm you up socially and verbally so you hit the ground running in any social situation.

It will teach you to be comfortable and happy with how your voice sounds, and greatly increase your social confidence.

Conclusion

If there's anything that you should take away from this book, I hope it's that social fluency is a daily choice we all make… and it's that choice that leads to genuine social habits that will improve your presence and relationships exponentially.

We have 100% control over the response we get from the world, and it's a privilege that we shouldn't let fall by the wayside. The contrary being that you only take what the world gives you… and I should hope that none of you live your life on such passive terms.

Grasping true social fluency, as with mastering anything, is a lifelong process. I believe that the set of habits and mindsets I have presented in this book can serve as the foundation for a better, more socially successful you.

Remember that habits are more powerful than our willpower and discipline most of the time. Don't let this be your reality to ensure that you are that person that people look up to in social contexts.

Working a room, owning a conversation, being instantly likeable?

Simply inevitably side effects of the manifestation of your genuine social habits.

Sincerely,

Patrick King
Dating and Social Skills Coach
www.PatrickKingConsulting.com

P.S. If you enjoyed this book, please don't be shy and drop me a line, leave a review, or both! I love reading feedback, and reviews are the lifeblood of Kindle books, so they are always welcome and greatly appreciated.

Other books by Patrick King include:

CHATTER: Small Talk, Charisma, and How to Talk to Anyone http://www.amazon.com/dp/B00J5HH2Y6

MAGNETIC: How to Impress, Connect, and Influence http://www.amazon.com/dp/B00ON8WJKY

Cheat Sheet

1. <u>Social fluency is learned</u>. Positive social habits are learned by observation and pattern recognition, but you also have to ensure that you are modeling off positive behaviors.

2. <u>Overcoming your social fears and excuses</u>. Only you know deep inside whether the excuses for avoiding social situations are legitimate. Attempt to push through them because the consequences are never so bad, and you need exposure to build your social habits.

3. <u>Social body over mind</u>. If you go through the motions physically, your mind will start to believe your body and take note.

4. <u>Familiarity breeds social comfort</u>. If you can familiarize with a social context, you have eliminated a large source of anxiety and can focus on the social task at hand.

5. <u>Turn social fluency on like a light switch</u>. Pair whatever triggers your social states with a physical action to call them up at any time.

6. <u>The buddy system isn't just for swimming</u>. Draft an accountability buddy for social situations and goals, and they will push you through your challenges to new heights.

7. <u>The barista is your guinea pig</u>. Practice your social skills with service people and see how you can improve with unlimited shots at the goal.

8. <u>Storytelling as influencing</u>. The act of storytelling contains all essential elements of influencing people, therefore influence people by telling great stories.

9. <u>Act familiar, become familiar</u>. If you act familiar and emphasize commonalities you have with others, they will more readily accept you and connect with you.

10. <u>Understand and take advantage of conversation patterns</u>. The vast majority of conversations follow the same script – re-write the script exactly how you want to.

11. <u>Conversations as pure entertainment</u>. Think outside the box and focus on the entertainment value of conversations – connection and influence are only a stone's throw away from that precursor.

12. <u>Be unapologetically you</u>. Don't try to be friends with everyone, just be your slightly polarizing self and find out who loves you for you.

13. <u>Figure out your social triggers</u>. Isolate the factors in people and situations that trigger your social moods and visualize them for on-demand social fluency.

14. <u>What you say doesn't really matter</u>. Genuine social interaction is all about the feeling and tone you convey about yourself, which is not imparted verbally.

15. <u>Condition emotional attraction</u>. If you come to represent positive vibes and just make people feel good about interacting with you, you will be sought out.

16. <u>Own group discussion dynamics</u>. Either focus on building rapport with your neighbors in a group, or act as a discussion leader in a literature class.

17. <u>Genuine social habits</u>. Take note of your negative social habits, the signals you send out, and avoid the negative spirals they cause.

18. <u>Take control of your feedback loops</u>. You can control the exact response you want back from the word, it's just a mindset of intentionality.

www.ingramcontent.com/pod-product-compliance
Lightning Source LLC
Chambersburg PA
CBHW051736170526
45167CB00002B/965